# Provinces and Territories of Canada

# YUKON

*— "Larger than Life" —*

Published by Weigl Educational Publishers Limited
6325 10 Street SE
Calgary, Alberta
T2H 2Z9

www.weigl.com

Library and Archives Canada Cataloguing in Publication data available upon request.
Fax 403-233-7769 for the attention of the Publishing Records department.

ISBN 978-1-55388-980-9 (hard cover)
ISBN 978-1-55388-993-9 (soft cover)

Printed in the United States of America
1 2 3 4 5 6 7 8 9 0  13 12 11 10 09

Editor: Heather C. Hudak
Design: Terry Paulhus

Every reasonable effort has been made to trace ownership and to obtain permission to reprint copyright material. The publishers would be pleased to have any errors or omissions brought to their attention so that they may be corrected in subsequent printings.

Weigl acknowledges Getty Images as one of its image suppliers for this title.
National Archives of Canada: pages 26, 31 top; Territorial Government of the Yukon: page 34 top.

All of the Internet URLs given in the book were valid at the time of publication. However, due to the dynamic nature of the Internet, some addresses may have changed, or sites may have ceased to exist since publication. While the author and publisher regret any inconvenience this may cause readers, no responsibility for any such changes can be accepted by either the author or the publisher.

We gratefully acknowledge the financial support of the Government of Canada through the Book Publishing Industry Development Program (BPIDP) for our publishing activities.

# Contents

# Yukon

The Yukon is one of Canada's three territories. It is located in the far northwest of the country, and is home to some of the most beautiful natural scenery in North America. In the Yukon, summer days are long and sunny, and the land is covered in colourful wildflowers. The long hours of summer sunshine in the North has earned the Yukon the nickname "Land of the Midnight Sun." The Yukon's landscape is both diverse and exciting. The territory is made up of towering mountain ranges, rolling plateaus, wide expanses of **tundra**, and rugged coastal areas. Outdoor enthusiasts from all over the world come to the Yukon to experience its amazing wilderness.

The Yukon is home to vast areas of rugged and untouched beauty.

Aboriginal Peoples live throughout the Yukon and make up about one-fourth of the territory's population.

The Yukon Territory was named after the large river running through the region. The Loucheux peoples called the river Yu-kun-ah, which means "Great River." Hudson's Bay Company fur trader John Bell first used the name "Yucon" for the region in 1846. Today, the region is referred to as both "the Yukon" and "Yukon."

The Yukon is roughly triangular in shape. It is bordered by Alaska in the west and southwest, British Columbia in the south, the Northwest Territories in the east, and the Beaufort Sea in the north. The territory includes Herschel Island, which lies just north of the mainland in the Beaufort Sea.

Aboriginal Peoples were the earliest inhabitants of the Yukon. They lived in the region many thousands of years ago, and were among the first peoples in North America. Today, some of the Aboriginal Peoples who live in the region are descendants of these early inhabitants. The Yukon's Aboriginal Peoples have a long and proud history. Their various cultures have a major influence on many aspects of daily life in the territory.

When gold was discovered in the Yukon in the late 19th century, the territory was changed forever. Thousands of people came to the area hoping to find their fortune. This was called the **Klondike Gold Rush**. The Gold Rush era resulted in the creation of settlements, roads, businesses, and many colourful stories about the people and events in the region.

Gold was the first important mineral resource discovered in the Yukon. In the twentieth century, other natural resources, such as zinc, lead, and natural gas, became important to the Yukon's economy. As well as the mining industry, tourism is an important source of revenue for the territory. Visitors are drawn to the territory's fascinating historical sites, beautiful natural areas, and exciting cultural festivals. The national parks, territorial parks, and historic sites in the Yukon are popular destinations. Yukoners and tourists enjoy many outdoor activities, such as snowmobiling, backpacking, and canoeing.

The Yukon's vast wilderness provides an excellent setting for all kinds of outdoor activity.

The Yukon is the fifth smallest political region in Canada. Only the four Atlantic provinces—Nova Scotia, Newfoundland, New Brunswick, and Prince Edward Island—are smaller.

The Yukon became a separate territory on June 13th, 1898. Before then, it was part of the Northwest Territories.

The Yukon lies farther west than any other part of Canada.

The Yukon shares more than 1,040 kilometres of border with Alaska.

The Yukon covers 483,450 square kilometres.

Whitehorse is the capital city of the territory.

The Yukon's nickname, "Land of the Midnight Sun," comes from the fact that above the **Arctic Circle**, the sun shines for most of the day and night during the summer months. During the winter, the sun barely shines at all.

# LAND AND CLIMATE

Due to the darkness, winter in the Yukon is the best time to view the northern lights.

The Yukon landscape is made up of three main kinds of terrain. There are mountains, plateaus, and coastal tundra. Most of the territory lies in the Western Cordillera, a great mountain chain that forms the western rim of North America. The Saint Elias mountain range in the southwest is the largest range in the territory. High plateaus separate the mountain ranges, and the area's powerful rivers have carved numerous valleys.

Most of the Yukon is covered by **permafrost**, ground that remains frozen throughout the year. Permafrost lies just beneath a thin upper layer of ground called the active layer. This active layer usually thaws in summer. When the active layer thaws, the frozen ground does not absorb the water, resulting in many swamps and bogs.

The Yukon River is the second longest in Canada and the fifth longest in North America.

Canada's highest mountain, Mount Logan, is part of the Saint Elias mountain range. Mount Logan's highest point is 5,959 metres above sea level.

The Yukon is situated in the subarctic zone. This means that it is colder than most other regions in Canada. Its summers are short and usually cool, but sometimes temperatures can reach a balmy 25° Celsius.

The Yukon's winters are long and cold because the territory is so far north, and the mountains keep the warmer Pacific Ocean air from reaching the region. Winter temperatures in the Yukon usually range from 4°C to –50°C.

GET THE FACTS

The Saint Elias Mountains have vast ice fields that are remnants of the last Ice Age.

Yukon receives between 23 and 43 centimetres of precipitation each year.

There are 13 lakes in the Yukon. The largest lakes are the Teslin, Kluane, Laberge, Aishihik, and Tagish.

The Arctic Circle goes through the northern part of the Yukon Territory.

One of the lowest recorded temperatures in North America was recorded in the western Yukon in 1947. It was –63°C.

# NATURAL RESOURCES

Placer mining takes place when gold is extracted from dry riverbeds or deltas. This type of formation is common in many parts of the Yukon.

Ever since gold was first discovered in the territory, the Yukon economy has been centred on its mineral resources. **Prospectors** started the mining industry in the territory when they began digging for gold.

After World War II, other minerals, including copper, zinc, lead, silver, and asbestos, began to attract miners. The Yukon is still rich in mineral resources, and mining remains an important activity throughout the territory.

## KEEP CONNECTED

To learn more about the rich history of mining in the Yukon, visit www.emr.gov.yk.ca/mining/history.html.

Forests cover about 57 percent of the Yukon's total land area.

The official gemstone of the Yukon is lazulite.

The Yukon's abundance of wildlife was the reason for the territory's thriving fur trade in the 1800s. Today, the territory's animals attract hunters. As well, the many lakes and rivers are full of fish. While there is little commercial fishing in the Yukon, many people fish as a means of obtaining food.

GET THE FACTS

Despite the Yukon's rugged and challenging terrain, mining activity in the territory is abundant. Iron has been extracted from open-pit mines.

Less than 2 percent of land in the Yukon is suitable for farming.

In coastal areas, which are above the **tree line** in the Yukon, driftwood is the only wood available for burning and for building.

The Yukon gets most of its energy from two **hydroelectric** facilities.

Eighty percent of the Yukon is wilderness area.

# PLANTS AND ANIMALS

Fireweed is the official flower of the territory. Although trees do not grow above the tree line, shrubs and wildflowers are still plentiful.

Wild pasque flowers can be seen in the territory. They are regarded as a sign that spring has finally arrived.

Much of the Yukon is covered in subarctic **boreal forest**, which includes pine, poplar, aspen, and birch trees. Most of the trees and plants in the Yukon are smaller than similar species elsewhere in Canada. They also grow more slowly as a result of the territory's climate. About 1,300 different types of wildflowers, shrubs, and ferns grow in the region. The pasque flower, also called the Yukon crocus, is the first flower to appear through the melting snow in the spring. Blue lupin, Jacob's ladder, arctic poppies, wild roses, and arctic cotton grass are among the many plants that grow in the territory.

In the summer, wild berries provide food for both people and animals. Cranberries, blueberries, strawberries, raspberries, cloudberries, and crowberries are among the many types of edible berries in the Yukon. Bears eat soapberries to fatten up for the winter.

Seals, walruses, and whales live off the Yukon coast.

The Yukon is home to a tremendous variety of animals. Beavers, martens, minks, and arctic and red foxes can all be found in the territory. Wolves, hares, otters, lynxes, wolverines, coyotes, moose, muskoxen, bison, mountain goats, elk, and Dall's sheep also live in the Yukon. All three types of bears common to North America—the American black bear, the grizzly bear, and the polar bear—can be found in the territory.

## KEEP CONNECTED

For information about viewing wildlife in the Yukon, check out www.environmentyukon.gov.yk.ca/ wildlifebiodiversity/wildlifeviewing.php.

The Yukon is home to one of North America's largest populations of Dall's sheep.

The raven is the Yukon's official bird.

Many birds spend all or part of the year in the Yukon. Bald eagles, golden eagles, hawks, owls, geese, loons, and ducks all live in the region. Sparrows, ravens, woodpeckers, finches, and jays are also common.

The area's lakes, rivers, and seas are home to many different species of fish, including rainbow trout, lake trout, whitefish, arctic char, and several types of salmon.

**GET THE FACTS**

There are 6,000 to 7,000 grizzly bears in the Yukon.

Forest fires, often started by lightning, destroy millions of square kilometres of forest each year in the Yukon.

The Yukon's forests are among the most remote and slowest-growing in the country.

Dall's sheep sheep have a coat that is suited for a cold climate. In the winter, their coats will often grow to more than 5 centimetres in length.

The Yukon has more than 1,000 species of plants.

A herd of 128,000 barren-ground caribou spend part of the year in the Yukon.

# TOURISM

Dawson City was the capital of the Yukon from 1898 to 1953.

Tourism is big business in the Yukon. The major tourist season is from late May to late September. During that time, thousands of tourists travel to the Yukon, filling the hotels and keeping the restaurants busy. Many tourism-related businesses are closed for the remainder of the year. Visitors can learn more about the Yukon's colourful cultural life by exploring the territory's communities.

In Whitehorse, a number of museums document every part of the Yukon's past. The Yukon Transportation Museum shows moose skin boats, snowshoes, stagecoaches, dogsleds, and other early forms of northern transport. The MacBride Museum exhibits the territory's natural and cultural history, and the Old Log Church Museum displays the lives of early missionaries in the north.

In Dawson City, a number of historical sites depict the days of the Gold Rush. The Yukon's many parks provide tourists with excellent opportunities for hiking, mountain climbing, wildlife watching, and other outdoor pursuits.

The S.S. Klondike National Historic Site in Whitehorse displays one of the largest steamboats used on the Yukon River during the Gold Rush.

Kluane National Park is a UNESCO World Heritage Site.

There are three national parks in the Yukon. They are Ivvavik, Kluane, and Vuntut. Kluane National Park is one of the Yukon's most popular natural attractions. The park covers 22,015 square kilometres of breathtaking wilderness. Here, visitors can explore Canada's highest mountains and the largest non-polar ice field in the world.

## GET THE FACTS

The Sign Post Forest in Watson Lake is a collection of more than 40,000 signs.

Carl K. Lindley, a homesick Alaskan construction worker, erected the first sign, which pointed to his home town of Danville, Illinois, in 1942.

The Keno City Mining Museum has artifacts dating back to when Keno City was the largest silver producer in North America.

The Dawson City Museum has many exhibits and artifacts that date back to the height of the Gold Rush.

# INDUSTRY

Visitors to the Yukon can see recreation of 19th-century gold mining camps.

The mining industry has long been a central part of the Yukon's economy. Mining first became profitable in the territory when the discovery of gold brought thousands of fortune-seekers to the area in the late 1800s. Today, many other minerals are actively explored and mined in the Yukon. Lead, zinc, and silver are all produced at Keno Hill, near Mayo. These high-grade ores are then transported south to British Columbia for **smelting**.

Other resources that hold great future potential for the territory are oil and gas. In 1998, the federal government gave the Yukon government control of the territory's petroleum reserves. There is already one producing gas field in the southeast area of the Yukon.

There are about 2,100 businesses currently operating in the Yukon.

Dempster Highway was Canada's first all-weather road to cross the Arctic Circle.

Tourism is another major industry in the Yukon. It earns the territory around $124 million every year. About 70 percent of the Yukon's working population is employed in jobs related to tourism. Also, the construction of the Alaska Highway during World War II helped make the Yukon more accessible for tourists and contributed to the expansion of many businesses. Then, in 1979, the Canadian government opened the Dempster Highway, east of Dawson City.

**GET THE FACTS**

Commercial gardening is an important industry in the Yukon despite the territory's short growing season.

Plants in greenhouses grow well during the long daylight hours of the summer months.

Outfitting and tour companies in the Yukon generate substantial income for the territory every year.

Forestry is becoming an im[portant] industry for the Yuko[n] territory's high-[?] popular aro[?]

# GOODS AND SERVICES

important
...The
...ality wood is
...und

The Yu...
as well as ly...

20 PROVINCES

...on industry. Marten,
...eir fur.

ANADA

Northern pike are fished in the Yukon.

Many Yukoners work in one of the territory's manufacturing industries. These industries include mineral refining, printing, and sawmilling. Wood products are among the leading manufactured goods in the Yukon. Locally-made furniture and lumber is sold outside the territory. As well, many local artisans produce beautiful crafts that are sold to the tourists who visit the territory. Some of these goods are also exported to other parts of the world.

The Yukon also produces some farm products, such as livestock, vegetables, and grains. Crops are grown and farm animals are raised mostly for the local market. Fish are important goods for Yukoners. There is some fish processing in the territory, and a small **aquaculture** industry also exists. Like farming, fishing is done mostly for local markets or for personal consumption. Many remote communities in the Yukon rely heavily on fishing, hunting, and trapping for survival.

Almost one-third of all retail spending in the Yukon is in grocery stories.

Most employed Yukoners work in one of the territory's many service industries. These are industries that provide some sort of assistance to others. People who work in service industries include administrative assistants, waiters, government workers, and doctors.

Many Yukoners work for one of the three levels of government represented in the territory—federal, territorial, or municipal. Other Yukoners work in the retail industry, selling locally-made goods and imports to residents or tourists.

## KEEP CONNECTED
Information about the Yukon's goods and services, as well as places to visit and much more, can be found at **http://travelyukon.com**.

There are 28 public schools in the territory.

Another important service is education. Although it is a territory rather than a province, the Yukon is still responsible for its own education system. Public school education is administered by four regional superintendents. Yukon College, a junior college based in Whitehorse, is the only post-secondary school in the territory. The college offers a variety of programs and has campuses in other communities.

GET THE FACTS

Stores in Dawson City provide Yukoners and visitors with all kinds of supplies and momentos.

Yukon College's main campus is located at Yukon Place, in Whitehorse.

The Yukon has six radio stations and two television stations.

The Yukon produces about 15 different newspapers. These include dailies, weeklies, monthlies, and annual publications.

The Royal Canadian Mounted Police maintain law and order in the territory.

# FIRST NATIONS

Many thousands of years ago, Russia and Alaska were connected by a land bridge. Hunters made use of this land bridge while following bison and woolly mammoth from Asia, through Alaska, to the Yukon.

Anthropologists estimate there were anywhere from 6,000 to 40,000 Aboriginal Peoples living in the Yukon region prior to European settlement. These peoples spoke languages from two main language groups: the Athapaskan group and the Tlingit. There were five major groups of Athapaskans: the Gwich'in, Han, Tutchone, Kaska, and Tagish. Each group lived in a different part of the Yukon. In the 1800s, a group of First Nations from Alaska, the Tlingit, moved into the southern Yukon.

About 500 western Arctic Inuit—called Inuvialuit—lived on the coast around 1890. By the 1920s, most of the Yukon Inuvialuit were either dead from diseases carried by whalers from the United States, or had moved eastward in Canada.

Early Aboriginal Peoples made use of all parts of the animals they hunted. The hides were tanned and used to make clothing. Other body parts were used to make snowshoes and tools. Any leftover meat was smoked to preserve it for later use.

Today, many Aboriginal Peoples in the Yukon work to preserve the traditional ways of their ancestors through language, music, and art.

The early Aboriginal Peoples of the Yukon lived in small groups of 20 to 25 people. In order to survive in their harsh environment, they had to work together. They caught fish during the summer, drying much of it for use during the cold winter months. They also gathered berries and hunted small mammals, such as hares. In the fall, they would hunt larger animals, like caribou. In the wintertime, they lived near lakes, catching small mammals and fishing through holes they made in the ice.

The **potlatch** is a festive Aboriginal ceremony involving dancing, feasting, and the giving of gifts. Early missionaries to the Yukon felt that the potlatch was an evil celebration. The Canadian government made potlatches illegal in 1884. In 1951, the government declared that potlatches were no longer illegal. Aboriginal Peoples in the Yukon continue to hold potlatches today.

# EXPLORERS

On his third trip to the Arctic, in 1845, John Franklin and his men died tragically when their ships became stuck in the icy waters.

European explorers did not arrive in the Yukon area until the first half of the 19th century. Many entered the region while searching for the Northwest Passage, a short-cut trading route linking the Atlantic and Pacific Oceans.

Sir John Franklin, a British sea captain, was among the most famous of these explorers. He and his crew were probably the first to reach the Yukon region when they visited Herschel Island in 1825. Franklin made three trips to explore the Arctic.

In the 1840s, the Hudson's Bay Company sent people to the Yukon to establish the fur trade in the region. John Bell explored the Yukon interior via the Porcupine and Yukon Rivers, and Robert Campbell sailed westward from the Mackenzie River system to explore the Pelly River.

## KEEP CONNECTED

To learn more about the Yukon's early inhabitants and explorers, surf to www.collectionscanada.gc.ca/confederation/023001-2260-e.html.

The Hudson's Bay Company set up trading posts across Canada.

In 1848, Campbell established a fur trading post at Fort Selkirk, near the junction of the Yukon and Pelly Rivers. Other posts, including Fort Frances and Fort Yukon, were also set up during the 1840s. However, the fur trade in the Yukon was not a huge success. The region was too remote, and transporting furs to Britain took a great deal of time and trouble. Trading posts were often abandoned just a few years after being established.

GET THE FACTS

Reverend Robert McDonald, who came to the Yukon in 1862 and stayed for 40 years, translated the Bible into the Gwich'in language.

At the end of the 19th century, some seamen hunted whales along the north coast, but they did not settle in the area.

The British Navy mapped most of the Arctic islands and straits while searching for John Franklin and his crew.

When Russia sold Alaska to the United States in 1867, the Americans claimed that Fort Yukon was in U.S. territory. The fort was moved further inland, but later abandoned.

# EARLY SETTLERS

The Yukon became a separate territory on June 13, 1898. It was established to help protect Canadian land from the flood of American prospectors during the Gold Rush.

Gold was discovered in a tributary of the Klondike River in August 1896, making the Yukon famous around the world.

In the 1860s, Britain bought the Yukon back from the Hudson's Bay Company. The British feared that the United States might try to take control of the area, and they wanted to prevent this from happening.

Canada became an independent nation in 1867, and the Yukon became part of the Northwest Territories in 1895. At that time, there were only about 1,000 people living in the region. Early gold prospectors moved into the area in the 1860s and 1870s. Some gold was found during those years, but not enough to generate worldwide interest.

In 1896, an enormous amount of gold was discovered in the Klondike River, and the Gold Rush began. By 1898, up to 100,000 people came from across North America and Europe in the hope of finding their fortune in the North.

At the height of the Klondike Gold Rush, Dawson City was known as "Paris North."

The North-West Mounted Police required that each prospector going through the Chilkoot Pass have enough supplies to last one year in the wilderness. This amounted to about 800 kilograms of supplies. Prospectors had to make several trips through the pass to carry their supplies.

Prior to the Gold Rush, Dawson City was home to very few people. In May 1898, it became the largest city in North America west of Winnipeg and north of San Francisco. About 40,000 people lived in the city, and many hotels, casinos, saloons, and dance halls opened.

The Klondike Gold Rush was instrumental in developing the Yukon. The White Pass and Yukon Railway was created to help people travel to the region.

After the Gold Rush died down, the population of the Yukon decreased quickly. The construction of the Alaska Highway during World War II again brought people to the area.

Once construction of the Alaska Highway was completed, access to the Yukon became much more convenient.

Thousands of Canadian and American construction workers came to help build the highway. Businesses sprung up to provide services to the workers. Whitehorse, which is on the Alaska Highway route, became the largest community in the territory.

## GET THE FACTS

Herschel Island was named after Sir John Herschel, a well-known chemist and astronomer. The Inuvialuit people who live in the area have always called the island Qikiqtaruk, which means "it is island."

In 1900, a railway was built between Whitehorse and Skagway, Alaska.

Skookum Jim, Tagish Charlie, and George Carmack are all credited with finding the gold that began the Klondike Gold Rush.

Visitors interested in panning for gold are still likely to find gold flakes and nuggets among the gravel from the territory's creeks.

Before 1896, most of the residents of the Yukon were First Nations.

The Yukon remained a fairly peaceful region during the Gold Rush thanks to the work of the North-West Mounted Police.

Several gold-mining centres were set up in the Yukon during the late 19th century. Many of these centres lasted only a brief period as prospectors and businesspeople moved through the area in search of gold.

# POPULATION

Whitehorse is the transportation, communication, and distribution centre of the Yukon.

The Yukon has a population of more than 30,000. About two-thirds of these people live in the territory's only city— Whitehorse. Other Yukoners live in Dawson City, Watson Lake, or Haines Junction, which are the only three towns in the territory. The Yukon also has four villages, thirteen unincorporated communities, and eight rural communities. Much of the territory remains unpopulated.

Most Yukoners come from other parts of Canada. Many of these people come to the Yukon because of the high wages. They often plan to stay in the territory for only a short time to make money. Nearly half of the Yukon's people have some British ancestry, and about 25 percent have Aboriginal ancestry.

## KEEP CONNECTED

Information about the City of Whitehorse can be found by visiting www.city.whitehorse.yk.ca.

At the height of the Gold Rush, there were well over 40,000 people living in the Yukon. By 1901, that number had decreased to 27,219. Ten years later, the Yukon had a population of only 8,512.

## Yukon population increase or decrease from 2007 to 2008 by age group

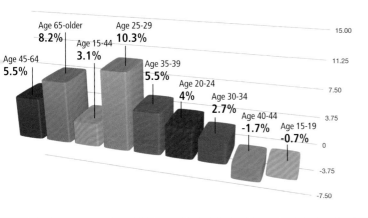

Age 65-older **8.2%**
Age 15-44 **3.1%**
Age 25-29 **10.3%**
Age 45-64 **5.5%**
Age 35-39 **5.5%**
Age 20-24 **4%**
Age 30-34 **2.7%**
Age 40-44 **-1.7%**
Age 15-19 **-0.7%**

15.00
11.25
7.50
3.75
0
-3.75
-7.50

For six years, the Yukon's population decreased. This changed, however, in 2003, when the population began to climb. In 2008, the population increased by 1,102 to a total of 33,378 people.

Old Crow is the most northerly, and the most isolated, community in the Yukon. It is also the largest exclusively Aboriginal settlement in the Yukon.

Dawson City was made a National Historic Site because of the lively and important role it played in the territory's history.

Whitehorse is the most westerly city in Canada.

Most of the residents in Old Crow practise the traditional hunting and fishing methods of their ancestors.

# POLITICS AND GOVERNMENT

The Yukon's territorial government meets at the Legislative Building in Whitehorse.

The Yukon territorial government consists of three separate bodies. A Legislative Assembly, consisting of 17 elected members, governs the Yukon Territory. The main executive body is the Cabinet, or executive council, made up of members of the Legislative Assembly. A premier is the head of the Cabinet. All members of the Legislative Assembly are elected to four-year terms.

The judicial branch of government includes the court of appeal, which is the territory's highest court and hears appeals from lower courts. The Supreme Court hears major civil and criminal cases and is made up of two resident and forty nonresident justices. The Yukon territorial court has three resident and 14 nonresident judges.

The Yukon's local government is much the same as local governments throughout the country. A mayor and council run the towns and Whitehorse. The federal government appoints a commissioner to be in charge of federal interests in the territory.

The Yukon Territory elects one member to the federal Parliament in Ottawa. The member of Parliament (MP) serves a term of up to five years. One senator represents the Yukon in parliament.

The Yukon has had elected representatives in the territorial government since 1900.

The Yukon Progressive Conservative Party was the first political party elected to run the territorial government.

In 1991, the Yukon Progressive Conservative Party, who wanted to set themselves apart from the federal PC party, became the Yukon Party. Today, the Yukon Party, the Yukon Liberal Party, and the Yukon New Democratic Party are the three major political parties in the territory.

# CULTURAL GROUPS

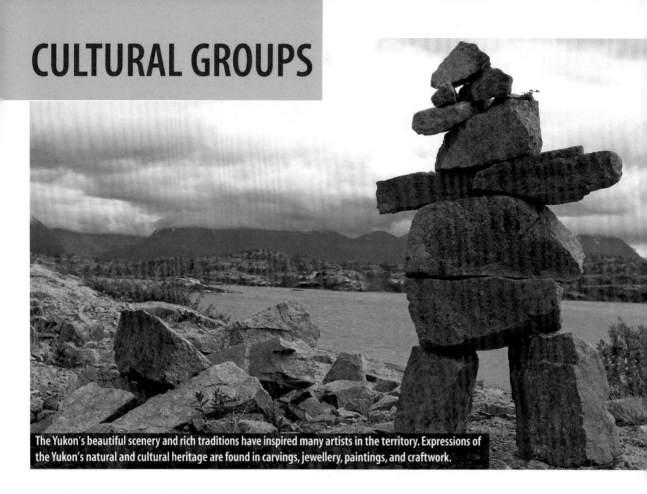

The Yukon's beautiful scenery and rich traditions have inspired many artists in the territory. Expressions of the Yukon's natural and cultural heritage are found in carvings, jewellery, paintings, and craftwork.

Aboriginal Peoples have contributed greatly to the Yukon's cultural atmosphere. Numerous museums, festivals, and other cultural events help to keep Aboriginal culture alive in the territory. Artwork, music, storytelling, and poems are just a few of the important cultural expressions of the Yukon's Aboriginal Peoples.

Throughout their history, the Aboriginal Peoples of the Yukon have developed beautiful artwork and crafts. Early clothing was decorated with items such as beads, porcupine quills, seeds, and moose hair. The Yukon's Aboriginal Peoples also had a tradition of carving crests and images of the animals representing different groups. These images were embroidered on clothes and painted on walls, boats, and drums. Today, the Yukon has 14 Aboriginal groups. Eight different traditional languages are spoken in the territory—seven Athapaskan languages and one Tlingit.

Many Aboriginal artists make carvings from stone, antlers and other animal bones. They also make jewellery, moccasins, masks, beadwork, and paintings.

Many of the Yukon's Aboriginal Peoples are skilled in unique craftmaking. Qiviuq is the craft of spinning wool from the under hair of a muskox. Caribou tufting is the shaping of caribou hair into designs and sewing the tufts of hair onto fabric as decoration.

Different museums and festivals in the Yukon celebrate other aspects of the territory's rich history. The Gold Rush was the single most important event in the history of the Yukon. Many museums

Visitors to Bonanza Creek can learn more about the area's Gold Rush by taking part in traditional panning and gold-seeking methods.

and annual festivals celebrate the customs of the Gold Rush era. Visitors can learn how gold was panned at several places in the Yukon. The Klondike Visitors Association has a site on Bonanza Creek, where the Gold Rush first began. Panning involves scooping up gravel from the bottom of a stream in a large metal pan. After rotating the pan underwater for several minutes, the gravel is drained off. Any pieces of heavy gold sink to the bottom of the pan.

The Yukon Sourdough Rendezvous is celebrated each February in Whitehorse. The festival is a celebration of the nearing of the end of winter. People dress in costumes from the beginning of the 20th century. Sled dog races, fiddle contests, and dances are among the events. The Yukon also holds a number of festivals related to the Klondike Gold Rush. One of the most popular is Discovery Days, held every August in Dawson City. Festivities include a parade, huge picnics, and raft races.

# ARTS AND ENTERTAINMENT

The Yukon International Storytelling Festival has been held every year since 1988. Yukon Aboriginal storytellers are joined by storytellers from around the world who speak many different languages.

The Yukon has inspired several talented writers. Among the most prominent writers who have lived in the area are Robert Service and Jack London. In 1894, at the age of 20, Robert Service moved from England to Canada. He lived in Dawson City at the height of the Gold Rush. He captured the experience of the era in his poems and stories. "The Shooting of Dan McGrew" was about a real-life shootout in a Whitehorse saloon. Today, Robert Service's cabin is now part of the Dawson Historical Complex. Visitors to the cabin have the pleasure of listening to recitals of Service's poems and stories, which are performed daily. American writer Jack London also lived in the area during the Gold Rush. His experiences in the north inspired some of his writing, including one of his most famous books, *The Call of the Wild*.

One of Canada's most prominent and respected writers, Pierre Berton, is from the Yukon. Born in Whitehorse, he grew up in the territory, and has written many books about the area, including the well-received *Klondike*. In 1986, Berton was named Companion to the Order of Canada.  Pierre Berton's mother, Laura Berton, wrote a book called *I Married the Klondike*.

Yukoners who are interested in live theatre can take in a show at Whitehorse's Nakai Theatre or Dawson City's Palace Grand Theatre.

The Yukon has a number of popular music festivals that draw large crowds. The Frostbite Music Festival is held every February in Whitehorse. This festival combines lively concerts with dances, workshops, and children's activities to create a memorable experience for anyone who attends. The concerts feature both northern performers and other Canadian musicians. Later in the year, the Alsek Music Festival greets summer in Haines Junction. Yukon musicians and audiences sing and dance within a beautiful setting. Then, in July, the Dawson City Music Festival runs for three days under a sun that never sets. The festival has attracted talented musicians and is known nationally as "Canada's tiny, perfect festival."

GET THE FACTS

The MacBride Museum was named after William C. MacBride, who founded the Yukon Historical Society in 1950. The museum displays the cabin of Sam McGee, who was the subject of Robert Service's poem, "The Cremation of Sam McGee."

Artist Ted Harrison was born in England but spent many years in the Yukon. His bright paintings of the Yukon people and landscape have made him one of Canada's most beloved artists.

# SPORTS

Whitewater rafting is a common activity in the Yukon.

Skijoring, skiing while being pulled by a dog, is becoming a popular sport in the Yukon.

The wide expanses of land and diverse landscapes of the Yukon make the territory a perfect spot for many different activities. A variety of outdoor recreation is popular in the region. Many people fish, canoe, and boat in Yukon waters. Others hunt the big game that roam the territory's mountain wilderness. The Yukon also has excellent backpacking, hiking, camping, and horseback riding opportunities. Adventurous people participate in mountain biking, white-water rafting, river rafting, and mountain climbing.

Competitors in the Yukon Quest must travel 1,600 kilometres of difficult terrain during the coldest month of the year.

In the winter, cross-country skiing, snowshoeing, snowmobiling, and skating are all popular pastimes. Organized sports in the territory include hockey, curling, soccer, golf, volleyball, and tennis.

Dogsled racing is a popular sport in the territory's northern regions. The Yukon Quest is considered one of the most difficult sled dog races in the world. The race takes place between Whitehorse and Fairbanks, Alaska, every February. Fifty teams from around the world come to compete in the race. Teams have eight to 14 dogs and only one **musher**. Many different dog breeds are used, but Siberian huskies, malamutes, and husky-shepherd crosses are the most common.

## KEEP CONNECTED

The Arctic Winter Games are a biannual competition for athletes from northern Canada, the United States, Russia, and Greenland. For more information about this event, check out **www.arcticwintergames.org**.

The Great Klondike International Outhouse Race has been held every year since 1977 in Dawson City. Teams made up of five contestants, one sitting inside the outhouse and four carrying it, see who can complete the 3-kilometre course first. Competitors usually take turns sitting in the outhouse to get a rest during the race.

t takes about 10 to 14 days to finish the race, but each team is required to take a 36-hour break in Dawson City. The freezing temperatures of the north make the race even harder. Sometimes, temperatures can drop to as low as −62°C. The Yukon Quest begins in Whitehorse in odd-numbered years and in Fairbanks during even-numbered years. However, in 1998, the race began in Whitehorse to commemorate the **centennial** of the 1898 Klondike Gold Rush.

The Chilkoot Trail is a three-to-five-day backpacking trip for experienced trekkers.

Each year, contestants in the NMI Mobility Yukon River Bathtub Race, race down the Yukon River.

Whitehorse has a Triple-A hockey team called the Huskies.

The Klondike Trail of 1898 International Road Relay is a foot-race over 176 kilometres.

Kayak and canoe enthusiasts demonstrate their skills at Whitehorse's annual Whitewater Rodeo.

Every January, athletes compete in the Alcan 200 International Snowmachine Race, which runs through Alaska and the Yukon. Racers travel at speeds of more than 160 kilometres per hour over a 296-kilometre route. This is considered the world's longest snowmachine race.

# CANADA

Canada is a vast nation, and each province and territory has its own unique features. This map shows important information about each of Canada's 10 provinces and three territories, including when they joined Confederation, their size, population, and capital city. For more information about Canada, visit **http://canada.gc.ca**.

### Alberta
**Entered Confederation:** 1905
**Capital:** Edmonton
**Area:** 661,848 sq km
**Population:** 3,632,483

### British Columbia
**Entered Confederation:** 1871
**Capital:** Victoria
**Area:** 944,735 sq km
**Population:** 4,419,974

### Manitoba
**Entered Confederation:** 1870
**Capital:** Winnipeg
**Area:** 647,797 sq km
**Population:** 1,213,815

### New Brunswick
**Entered Confederation:** 1867
**Capital:** Fredericton
**Area:** 72,908 sq km
**Population:** 748,319

### Newfoundland and Labrador
**Entered Confederation:** 1949
**Capital:** St. John's
**Area:** 405,212 sq km
**Population:** 508,990

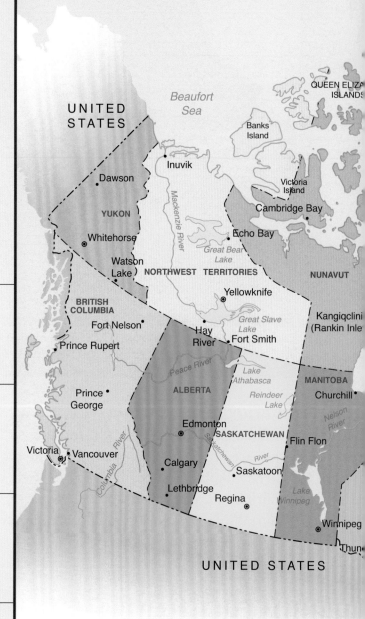

## SYMBOLS OF THE YUKON

**FLAG**

**COAT OF ARMS**

**FLOWER**
**Fireweed**

## Northwest Territories

**Entered Confederation:** 1870
**Capital:** Yellowknife
**Area:** 1,346,106 sq km
**Population:** 42,940

## Nova Scotia

**Entered Confederation:** 1867
**Capital:** Halifax
**Area:** 55,284 sq km
**Population:** 939,531

## Nunavut

**Entered Confederation:** 1999
**Capital:** Iqaluit
**Area:** 2,093,190 sq km
**Population:** 531,556

## Ontario

**Entered Confederation:** 1867
**Capital:** Toronto
**Area:** 1,076,395 sq km
**Population:** 12,986,857

## Prince Edward Island

**Entered Confederation:** 1873
**Capital:** Charlottetown
**Area:** 5,660 sq km
**Population:** 140,402

## Quebec

**Entered Confederation:** 1867
**Capital:** Quebec City
**Area:** 1,542,056 sq km
**Population:** 7,782,561

## Saskatchewan

**Entered Confederation:** 1905
**Capital:** Regina
**Area:** 651,036 sq km
**Population:** 1,023,810

## Yukon

**Entered Confederation:** 1898
**Capital:** Whitehorse
**Area:** 482,443 sq km
**Population:** 33,442

**BIRD**
Raven

**TREE**
Subalpine fir

**GEM**
Lazulite

# BRAIN TEASERS

Test your knowledge of the Yukon by trying to answer these boggling brain teasers!

**1** **Make a Guess**

How did the city of Whitehorse get its name?

**2** **True or False?**

Mount Logan, in Kluane National Park, is part of the Saint Elias mountain range.

**3** **True or False?**

Whitehorse is the most westerly community in Canada.

**4** **True or False?**

Dempster Highway was Canada's first all-weather road to cross the Arctic Circle.

**5** **Make a Guess**

What community was the capital of the Yukon before Whitehorse was made capital in 1953?

**6** **True or False?**

Kluane National Park is a UNICEF visitor centre.

**7** **True or False?**

The crow is the Yukon's official bird.

**8** **Multiple Choice**

Where is the Great Klondike International Outhouse Race held?
a. Dawson City
b. Whitehorse
c. Watson Lake
d. Faro

# MORE INFORMATION

## GLOSSARY

**aquaculture:** fish farming

**Arctic Circle:** the line of latitude running through the northern hemisphere at about 66°33' North

**boreal forest:** a large area in the northern hemisphere covered mainly in trees including pine, spruce, fir, birch, and poplar

**centennial:** a 100th anniversary

**hydroelectric:** electricity generated by moving water

**Klondike:** a region of the Yukon Territory near the Klondike River

**musher:** a person who navigates dog sleds

**permafrost:** permanently frozen ground

**potlatch:** a celebration held by certain First Nations groups. Depending on the group, potlatches may be held to celebrate marriages or deaths.

**prospectors:** people who explore a region for precious minerals such as gold

**smelting:** melting ore to obtain metal

**tree line:** a line of latitude and altitude beyond which trees will not grow

**tundra:** an Arctic or subarctic plain with a permanently frozen subsoil

## BOOKS

Aspen-Baxter, Linda. *Canadian Sites and Symbols: Yukon*. Calgary: Weigl Educational Publishers Limited, 2004.

Ostopowich, Melanie. *Canadian Geographic Regions: The Cordillera*. Calgary: Weigl Educational Publishers Limited, 2006.

Parker, Janice. *Canada's Land and People: Yukon*. Calgary: Weigl Educational Publishers Limited, 2008.

Tomljanovic, Tatiana. *Linking Canadian Communities: Mining*. Calgary: Weigl Educational Publishers Limited, 2008.

## WEBSITES

**The Yukon government**
www.gov.yk.ca

**Touring the Yukon**
www.touryukon.com

**Yukon Web**
www.yukonweb.com

Some websites stay current longer than others. To find information on the Yukon, use your Internet search engine to look up such topics as "Whitehorse," "Klondike," "Dawson City," or any other topic you wish to research.

# INDEX